IN THEIR OWN WORDS

THE VIETNAM WAR

A Primary Source History

Andrew Mason

GARETH**STEVENS**

PUBLISHING

A Member of the WRC Media Family of Companies

KEY TO SYMBOLS
The following symbols highlight the sources of material from the past.

FILM EXCERPT
Primary source material from a movie about the subject matter.

GOVERNMENT DOCUMENT
Text from an official government document.

INTERVIEW/BOOK EXTRACT
Text from an interview or book.

SONG EXCERPT/POEM
Text from songs or poems about the subject matter.

LETTER
Text from a letter written by a participant in the events.

NEWSPAPER ARTICLE
Extracts from newspapers of the period.

OFFICIAL SPEECH
Transcribed words from official government and other speeches.

PLAQUE/INSCRIPTION
Text from plaques or monuments erected in memory of events in this book.

TELEGRAM
Text from a telegram sent to or by a participant in the events.

Cover photos:
Top: *President Lyndon B. Johnson was the major U.S. leader during the Vietnam War.*
Bottom: *North Vietnamese troops resting during the 1968 Tet Offensive, one of the war's bloodiest periods.*

CONTENTS

Above: *This map shows the locations of the major battles of the Vietnam War.*

Below: *The country of Vietnam is located in southeast Asia.*

The Vietnam War was the most unpopular war the United States has ever fought, and it is the only war the country has ever lost. Almost sixty thousand Americans lost their lives in the jungles of Vietnam while millions of Vietnamese from both sides perished. The cost of the war ran into hundreds of billions of dollars for the United States, and it crippled the Vietnamese economy. The Vietnam War has colored U.S. foreign policy ever since, while Vietnam has become isolated internationally. Decades later, the war still looms large in the memories of many people in the United States, Vietnam, and around the world.

The crisis in Vietnam erupted during the 1940s, when large numbers of Vietnamese rose up against their French rulers. Chaos in Vietnam was temporarily resolved by a conference held in Geneva, Switzerland, in 1954, that divided the country into the communist North Vietnam and the democratic South Vietnam. This division was only intended to be temporary, but elections to reunify Vietnam were never held, and many people in the West feared for the future of South Vietnam.

In the United States, president after president decided that South Vietnam must not be allowed to fall under the control of communists. Beginning in 1954, a U.S. presence was established in the country. At first, U.S. forces were there only as advisers, training South Vietnamese troops to defend themselves from attack. By 1965, however, they were taking part in a bitter military conflict that would last another eight years. During this time, almost sixty thousand U.S. soldiers were killed in the jungles of Vietnam, together with more than one million Vietnamese. In 1973, swayed by rising opposition to the war among the American people and the realization that this war in the jungles of Southeast Asia could not be won, U.S. leaders decided that South Vietnam would have to stand alone. Just two years after U.S. troops left the country, forces from Hanoi, the capital of North Vietnam, rumbled into the South Vietnamese cities of Saigon and Le Duan and declared the birth of a communist Republic of Vietnam. The U.S. nightmare had come true, and soon after, the countries of Laos and Cambodia, which border Vietnam, also became communist.

Above: The jungles of Vietnam were unusual terrain for most U.S. soldiers.

Left: Many U.S. troops did not have the equipment they needed to fight in the jungles of Vietnam.

Peace for Vietnam, however, was short-lived. The country was at war again almost immediately, after it invaded Cambodia in 1978 and installed a pro-Vietnamese party in power. The following year, Vietnam was at war with China, which, at the time, was backed by the United States. These wars, together with the damage caused during the war with the United States, have made, Vietnam, even today, one of the poorest countries in

Above: *South Vietnamese troops try to defend their capital, Saigon, from attack. By 1973, their battle was becoming increasingly desperate.*

the world. The damage to the prestige of the United States that resulted from its defeat on the battlefield was immense. U.S. administrations retaliated by freezing all trade and diplomatic relations between the two countries. The United States also aired its grievances on the international stage, blocking Vietnam's entry into the United Nations. Soldiers returning home from the war also faced serious problems. They were vilified by some members of the American public for what they believed was "doing their duty," many found it difficult to settle back into civilian life. Abused and discriminated against, many resorted to alcohol and drugs. Internationally, defeat in Vietnam may have made the United States more cautious about committing troops to conflicts. Its next major battle was not until the 1991 Gulf War.

Today, the scars of the war in Vietnam are beginning to fade. As the Cold War came to an end with the collapse of the Soviet Union, or USSR, and the Eastern Bloc, people began to think about reconciliation. United States president Bill Clinton began the process of restoring relations between the two countries in 1994. Today, hundreds of thousands of American tourists visit Vietnam each year. Many Vietnamese people who emigrated to the United States have brought up a generation of children in the United States. These Amerasian children are a living bond between the two countries. In Vietnam, also, thousands of children were

Left: *At the time that the war began, Vietnam was a poor country in which most people used traditional farming methods. Here, two girls farm a rice paddy.*

born as a result of relationships between U.S. soldiers and South Vietnamese women. Problems caused by the war, however, remain. Vietnam remains desperately poor, and citizens from South Vietnam who fought against the communists continue to suffer discrimination. In the United States, around one- quarter of all homeless people in the country are Vietnam veterans. Families in both the United States and Vietnam that lost loved ones during the conflict continue to grieve and will never forget their losses.

Above: *This garland is decorated with the colors of the Vietnamese flag. Street vendors in Hanoi, Vietnam, sell their wares to tourists from all over the world, including the United States.*

Right: *President Bill Clinton was in part responsible for the improving relations between Vietnam and the United States. In this photo, President Clinton is shown with Vietnam's prime minister, Phan Van Khai (far right), at a conference in Auckland, New Zealand, in 1998.*

For centuries, Vietnam had a tradition of rejecting foreign interference in its affairs. Conquered by the Chinese in 111 B.C., the people of Vietnam mounted several unsuccessful rebellions until, in A.D. 938, they regained their independence. Another period of Chinese rule in the fifteenth century failed to suppress the Vietnamese identity, and the country expanded its territory until Europeans arrived in the region in the nineteenth century.

Above: In the United States, anti-communist propaganda appeared on bubble-gum cards like the one above. Ho Chi Minh was portrayed as an evil man with a twisting, snarling face.

Right: Dr. Ho Chi Minh, president of North Vietnam, accepts applause during a visit to Delhi, India, in 1958.

"All men are created equal. They are endowed by their Creator with certain inalienable rights; among these are life, liberty, and the pursuit of happiness. Those are undeniable truths. . . . The French have fled, the Japanese have capitulated, Emperor Bao Dai has abdicated. Our people have broken the chains which for nearly a century have fettered us and have won independence for the Fatherland. The whole Vietnamese people, animated by a common purpose, are determined to fight to the bitter end against any attempt by the French colonialists to reconquer our country. We are convinced that the Allied nations, led by America, Britain, and the Soviet Union have acknowledged the principles of self-determination and the equality of nations . . . and will not refuse to acknowledge the independence of Vietnam. . . . The entire Vietnamese people are determined to mobilize all their physical and mental strength, to sacrifice their lives and property, in order to safeguard their independence and freedom."

Ho Chi Minh, declaring the independence of the Republic of Vietnam, September 2, 1945.

> "Vietnam must have a communist party ... so the peasantry will overthrow the French Imperialists, seize political power, and set up the dictatorship of peasants and workers in order to achieve a communist society."
>
> **Ho Chi Minh, in "The Communists Must Organize Themselves into a Single Party," 1929.**
>
> "First, you must understand that to gain independence from a great power like France is a formidable task that cannot be achieved without some outside help. ... One must gain it through organization, propaganda, training, and discipline."
>
> **Ho Chi Minh to U.S. intelligence officer Charles Fenn, 1945.**

FRENCH CONQUERORS

After repeated attempts, France finally gained control of Vietnam, Cambodia, and Laos (as French Indochina) by 1887. The French built railways, roads, hospitals, and schools, mainly in South Vietnam. It was not until the 1930s that an organized Vietnamese resistance to French control began to emerge. In 1929, the communist Ho Chi Minh (born Nguyen That Thanh) set up the Indo-Chinese Communist Party (ICP) in Hong Kong. In 1940, a Franco-Japanese agreement allowed Japan to occupy Vietnam during World War II. Ho Chi Minh returned to Vietnam in 1941, set up the Vietminh nationalist organization, and called for an uprising against the country's foreign rulers. This revolt forced the Vietnamese-born but Japanese-controlled emperor, Bao Dai, to abdicate. When Japan surrendered to the Allies on September 2, 1945, Ho declared the birth of the Democratic Republic of Vietnam. Any prospect of peaceful transition was

TIME LINE
11 B.C.—1930

111 B.C.
Kingdom of Vietnam conquered by China.

A.D. 939
Vietnamese people end Chinese rule.

1407–1428
Another brief period of Chinese rule in Vietnam.

1858
France attacks Vietnam and occupies Saigon.

FEBRUARY 1930
Vietnamese Communist party formed by Ho Chi Minh.

Below: *A French sergeant inspects his troops in Vietnam in 1950.*

Above: *Following the 1954 Geneva Conference, Vietnam was divided at the seventeenth parallel into North Vietnam and South Vietnam. An area referred to as the demilitarized zone, or DMZ, divided the two countries.*

soon dashed. In the aftermath of the Allied victory in World War II, Great Britain and China were given the task of accepting the Japanese surrender in Vietnam. Chinese troops moved into North Vietnam and British troops, supporting the French desire to again take control of Vietnam, arrived the South. There, they joined with French forces to drive Ho's forces out of Saigon. While British and Chinese forces left Vietnam in 1946, French forces stayed. They persuaded Bao Dai to return as leader of Vietnam, and between 1946 and 1954, French troops fought a vicious battle with the Vietminh for control of the country. In 1945, U.S. president Franklin D. Roosevelt was opposed to French claims in Vietnam, but by the end of the decade, the new climate of the Cold War made the United States place its support behind French efforts to drive out the Vietminh. Increasingly concerned about the spread of communism across the world—a fear that escalated when China and much of eastern Europe became communist—and believing that Ho Chi Minh was controlled by the Soviet Union, the United States began to view the future of Vietnam as critical. When U.S. president Dwight D. Eisenhower's refusal to support France led to France's defeat at Dienbienphu in 1954, the United States realized that it might have to become more directly involved in Vietnam if it was to prevent Vietnam from becoming communist.

Left: *The French presence in Vietnam was bitterly resented by much of the Vietnamese population.*

"You have a row of dominoes set up; you knock over the first one, and what will happen to the last one is that it will go over very quickly. ... Asia, after all, has already lost some four hundred fifty million of its people to the Communist dictatorship, and we simply can't afford greater losses... . But when we come to the possible sequence of events, the loss of Indochina, of Burma, of Thailand, of the Peninsula, and Indonesia following, now you begin to talk about areas that not only multiply the disadvantages that you would suffer through the loss of materials, sources of materials, but now you are talking about millions and millions of people. Finally, the geographical position achieved thereby does many things. It turns the so-called island defensive chain of Japan, Formosa [Taiwan], of the Philippines, and to the southward; it moves in to threaten Australia and New Zealand. It takes away, in its economic aspects, that region that Japan must have as a trading area or Japan, in turn, will have only one place in the world to go—that is, toward the Communist areas in order to live.... So, the possible consequences of the loss are just incalculable to the free world."

President Dwight D. Eisenhower's "Domino Theory" speech, presidential press conference, April 7, 1954.

THE GENEVA CONFERENCE

While the French were being defeated in Vietnam, a conference was being held in Geneva to try to determine the future of the country. On July 21, a cease-fire was signed that temporarily divided the country into North Vietnam and South Vietnam and delcared that elections would be held within two years in order to reunify the country. Under the terms of the agreement, Ho Chi Minh formed a government in the North, while the stocky, chain-smoking Ngo Dinh Diem was made South Vietnam's prime minister in June 1954. Diem did not want elections to be held, because he believed that Ho would win easily. He turned away from the French and toward the United States for support and reassurance. The formation of the South East Asia Treaty Organization (SEATO), in which the United States and a number of other countries agreed to protect South Vietnam from aggression, marked the beginning of the increase of U.S. involvement in Vietnam.

TOWARD CIVIL WAR

As it became obvious that elections to unify the two countries would never be held, the United States became determined to support Diem's government. By 1958, it had invested more than a billion dollars in the regime. Ngo Dinh Diem's Army of the Republic of Vietnam (ARVN) waged a brutal war on communists based in the south. In response, Ho Chi Minh's government in Hanoi decided it was time to strike back. Members of Ho's North Vietnamese Army (NVA) were sent into South Vietnam by a route through Cambodia and Laos known as the Ho Chi Minh trail. In 1960, communist supporters in the South formed the National Liberation Front (NLF), referred to by Diem as the Viet Cong, to organize resistance efforts. The People's Liberation Armed Forces (PLAF) was formed to run the military

Below: *An ARVN Radio Operator, pictured in 1958.*

TIME LINE
1941–1960

MAY 1941
Ho Chi Minh helps to form the Vietminh organization.

MARCH 1945
Japanese-French government appoints Emperor Bao Dai head of Vietnam.

SEPTEMBER 2, 1946
Ho Chi Minh declares Vietnamese independence.

MAY 7, 1954
Vietminh defeat the French at Dienbienphu.

JULY 21, 1954
Geneva Conference temporarily divides Vietnam.

OCTOBER 26, 1955
Ngo Dinh Diem appointed president of South Vietnam.

DECEMBER 20, 1960
National Liberation Front (NLF) formed in South Vietnam.

"I would like to be able to report . . . I saw all the signs of misery and oppression that have made my visits to East Germany like nightmare journeys to 1984. But it was not so. At first it was difficult for me, as it is for any Westerner, to conceive of a Communist government's genuinely 'serving the people.' I could hardly imagine a Communist government that was also a popular government. . . . But this is just the sort of government the palm-hut state actually was while the struggle with the French continued. The Vietminh could not possibly have carried on the resistance for one year, let alone nine years, without the people's strong, united support."

American Joseph Alsop's report for *The New Yorker*, 1955.

Above: *A South Vietnamese service medal awarded to foreign soldiers who served in the country after 1960.*

Below: *A U.S. army chief instructs South Vietnamese soldiers in boarding procedures for an airlift on a U.S. Army helicopter.*

"Five or six Viet Cong guys stopped my bus one morning to check the identity cards of the passengers. They dragged two men off the bus, and their chief said to them: 'We've been waiting for you. We've warned you many times to leave your jobs but you haven't obeyed. So now we must carry out the sentence.'

"They forced the two men to kneel by the roadside, and one of the Viet Cong guys chopped off their heads with a machete. They then pinned verdicts to their shirts saying that the murdered men were policemen. The verdicts had been written out beforehand. It was horrible to watch."

A bus driver from Long Khanh province, northeast of Saigon, 1959.

side of the NLF. Viet Cong members attempted to convert South Vietnamese citizens to their cause using a mixture of assistance and intimidation. They made brutal attacks on citizens who were suspected of collaborating with the government and the United States.

UNITED STATES ASSISTANCE

In 1961, as John F. Kennedy took office as president of the United States, U.S. aid to South Vietnam reached an unprecedented level. President Kennedy's commitment to Vietnam as a vital Cold War-battleground became clear when he told a reporter

from *The New York Times*, "Now we have a problem in making our power credible, and Vietnam is the place." U.S. Special Forces called Green Berets were sent to Vietnam to train Diem's South Vietnamese ARVN in guerrilla warfare, a type of fighting suited to the jungles of Vietnam. Civilian Irregular Defence Groups (CIDGs) were established to provide surveillance in the mountains, while twenty-six hundred settlements known as "strategic hamlets" were placed under the watch of armed guards. At the same time, the number of U.S. advisors in Vietnam soared from fewer than one thousand in 1961 to more than twelve thousand by the following year.

"I joined the anticolonial underground when I was in my teens. I needed an occupation so I could live unnoticed in the South. I decided to open a noodle-soup shop. It would be a great place to shelter revolutionaries on the run. . . .

"Most of my customers were U.S. diplomats, military brass, and soldiers. I'd be smiling and serving soup to the Americans downstairs while the high command upstairs was planning their victory over the United States."

Toai, a Viet Cong spy, speaking in 1991.

TIME LINE
1962—1963

"We are launched on a course from which there is no respectable turning back: the overthrow of the Diem government. There is no turning back because US prestige is already publicly committed to this end in large measure, and will become more so as the facts leak out. In a more fundamental sense, there is no turning back because there is no possibility, in my view, that the war can be won under a Diem administration."

Henry Cabot Lodge, August 29, 1963.

FEBRUARY 1962
Military Assistance Command Vietnam (MACV) is established by the United States to support South Vietnam.

MAY–AUGUST 1963
Diem faces angry protests by Buddhists after his police raid a pagoda they claimed was sheltering communists.

NOVEMBER 3, 1963
Diem is assassinated.

NOVEMBER 22, 1963
Kennedy is assassinated.

THE END OF DIEM

United States plans to protect South Vietnam were complicated by the fact that Diem was becoming increasingly unpopular with his own people. Diem, a Catholic, found his relations with South Vietnam's Buddhist majority increasingly strained. When he enforced a rule banning the display of religious flags during a Buddhist festival, Buddhists in the city of Hue took to the streets. Diem's troops responded by opening fire on the demonstrators. In response, a monk named Thich Quang Duc set himself on fire, grabbing headlines across the world. When news reached the United States that a military coup against Diem was planned for November 1, President Kennedy—realizing that Diem could not bring stability to Vietnam—decided not to intervene to protect him. On November 2, 1963, Diem and his brother Ngo Dinh Nhu were murdered by ARVN soldiers. Ironically, Kennedy was also assassinated less than three weeks later. With Kennedy's death, the question of how to handle Vietnam passed to Vice President Lyndon B. Johnson.

Below: *South Vietnamese soldiers wade into a canal to lure Viet Cong guerrillas from flooded paddies.*

 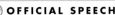

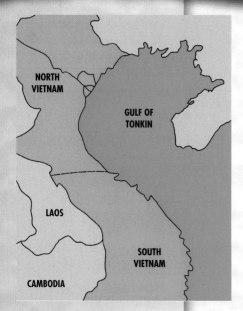

Above: *A map showing the Gulf of Tonkin, the location of the incident that sparked the escalation of the Vietnam conflict.*

Below: *President Lyndon B. Johnson pins medals on U.S. troops in recognition of deeds they performed in battle in Vietnam.*

With the assassinations of Diem and President Kennedy, civil unrest in South Vietnam, and the growing determination in the North to exploit these weaknesses, the prospect of a large-scale conflict in Vietnam had never been greater. The possibility of stationing U.S. forces in South Vietnam had become a reality.

THE GULF OF TONKIN INCIDENT

After the death of Diem, power in South Vietnam passed between several figures who seemed unable to restore order. The situation became even more critical because, beginning in December 1963, large numbers of troops were being sent South by Ho Chi Minh. To many Americans, it seemed that the South Vietnamese were unable or unwilling to fight this threat. It became increasingly clear to the new president, Lyndon B. Johnson, that the United States might have to commit more directly to the fight in Vietnam.

He would need, however, to find the justification for escalating the conflict. Such an opportunity presented itself in the summer of 1964. On August 2, North Vietnamese gunboats attacked a U.S. ship, the *Maddox*, employed on a spying mission off the coast of North Vietnam. This attack was recorded by photographers. Two days later, the *Maddox* and another U.S. boat, the *Turner Joy*, reported that they had been attacked during the night. There was no physical evidence of this attack, however, and many people—including the North Vietnamese authorities and several U.S. senators—claim that it never took place. After receiving the reports from the two

"As far as we can see, there are only three North Vietnamese boats, but we're having trouble with illumination. . . ."

Telephone call from U.S. admiral Grant Sharp, commander of the Pacific Fleet, to Air Force general David Burchinal of the Joint Chiefs of Staff, August 1964

"To this day I don't know what happened . . . in the Tonkin Gulf. . . . I think we may have made two serious misjudgments."

Former secretary of defense Robert McNamara speaking to General Giap in Hanoi, November 1995.

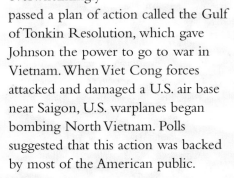

Above: *President Johnson authorized a massive bombing campaign in North Vietnam.*

U.S. boats, however, President Johnson asked Congress to support retaliatory strikes. On the basis of the information that was presented to them, Congress overwhelmingly passed a plan of action called the Gulf of Tonkin Resolution, which gave Johnson the power to go to war in Vietnam. When Viet Cong forces attacked and damaged a U.S. air base near Saigon, U.S. warplanes began bombing North Vietnam. Polls suggested that this action was backed by most of the American public.

GETTING IN DEEP

In February 1965, Viet Cong forces attacked a U.S. camp near Pleiku, killing eight soldiers and wounding more than one hundred others. A massive wave of air attacks on North Vietnam, known as Operation Rolling Thunder, was unleashed in retaliation. In the following spring, Johnson sent huge numbers of ground troops to Vietnam. On March 8, 1965, U.S. marines landed at Danang beach in central Vietnam, quickly followed by thousands more marines and support forces. Although it was never formally declared, the United States was now at war with North Vietnam. President Johnson convinced U.S. allies including Australia, South Korea,

and New Zealand to commit troops to the operation, but the United States supplied the overwhelming amount of manpower. By the end of the year, nearly 200,000 U.S. troops were in the country.

Hopes that Rolling Thunder would halt the flow of Northern forces into

"North Vietnamese naval units . . . in violation of international law, have deliberately and repeatedly attacked United States naval vessels . . . . The United States regards as vital to its national interest and to world peace the maintenance of international peace and security in South East Asia. Consonant with the Constitution of the United States and the Charter of the United Nations and in accordance with its obligations under the South East Asia Collective Defense Treaty, the United States is therefore prepared, as the president determines, to take all necessary steps, including the use of armed force, to assist any member or protocol state of the South East Asia Collective Defense Treaty requesting assistance in defense of its freedom."

The Gulf of Tonkin Resolution, August 1964.

TIME LINE
1963–1965

DECEMBER 1963
NVA units head south into South Vietnam.

JUNE 20, 1964
General William Westmoreland becomes head of MACV.

AUGUST 2, 1964
North Vietnamese attack on U.S. ship *Maddox*. A report of a further attack on the *Maddox* and on another ship, the *Turner Joy*, leads to proposal and passing of Gulf of Tonkin resolution.

FEBRUARY 7, 1965
NLF attacks U.S. military base in Pleiku.

FEBRUARY 13, 1965
President Johnson orders Operation Rolling Thunder.

FEBRUARY 8, 1965
First U.S. troops land in Vietnam.

Above: *The logo of the United States Marine Corps.*

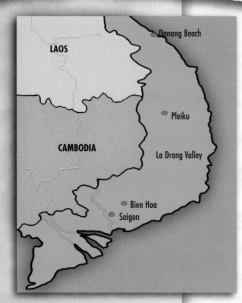

the South were ill-founded as large numbers of North Vietnamese troops continued to slip into South Vietnam. The influence of the Viet Cong was also growing. By the time the flamboyant but corrupt General Nguyen Van Thieu became head of state in South Vietnam in June 1965, it was estimated that they controlled up to 75 percent of the countryside of South Vietnam.

A SOLDIER'S LIFE

Boot camp was often a difficult experience for soldiers because instructors used relentless physical and psychological stress to mold their recruits into compliant soldiers. In contrast, life in Vietnam

for many soldiers was a mixture of extreme boredom punctuated by moments of terror and exhilaration. Life on the ground in Vietnam could be quite comfortable. Housing varied from flimsy plywood buildings to wooden cabins, and there was plenty of time for relaxation and entertainment. Rock and roll music was the soundtrack to soldiers' experiences in Vietnam, and alcohol and drugs were also readily available. Racism, which was a big part of life in the United States in the 1960s, usually evaporated in the muddy realities of the Vietnam jungle, where everyone had to live together and fight for each other. When soldiers engaged in combat, it was like nothing even seasoned soldiers had experienced. Apart from the difficulty of fighting in a landscape of vines

"Sunday, March 9, 1969

I'm sitting on the steps of our hooch looking out over the rice paddies and fields to the South. The Vietnamese are in the fields and paddies, working as they do every day. . . . I don't know how to describe Vietnam or what it's like for me being here. It's totally alien is all I can say. There is no time for me to be myself. And I hope the extent of the changes that it will make on me will be minimal, and when I come home I'll be able to forget that I was ever here and return to my old self. . . . My thoughts are mostly on Joanie and the time when I'll be home again. I think of our plans and what we will be doing once I get back to the States and can start living my life again. The first thing is for me to get back into school—that will be great. Next we will need some kind of a car and an apartment. Everything else will take care of itself.

Michael McAninch"

A letter home from U.S. marine Michael McAninch.

and swamps that was alien to U.S. forces, the ground was often booby trapped. One soldier described how the effect of the traps was "sometimes like paralysis . . . you walk like a wooden man . . . with your eyes pinned to the dirt, spine arched, and you are shivering, shoulders hunched."

LA DRANG

The first real battle between North Vietnamese and U.S. forces took place around the La Drang valley. When NVA forces attacked a camp in the South, the U.S. First Cavalry division and the ARVN drove them back to the valley. General Westmoreland ordered his troops to track down and kill the NVA soldiers. By the end of the confrontation, 305 U.S. troops and 3,561 NVA troops had been killed. Although La Drang seemed to be a victory for the United States, it made

Above: *Stores set up to serve U.S. soldiers were run by locals. Some of these locals were friendly to the Americans, but others resented their presence.*

the North Vietnamese move away from direct confrontations in favor of guerrilla warfare. The North Vietnamese leader General Vo Nguyen Giap's new tactic was to lure U.S. forces into the highlands where fighting was more difficult and more costly. The battle also showed that the North Vietnamese were willing to sustain casualty rates that the American public would never have been willing to tolerate.

TIME LINE
1965

APRIL 6, 1965
President Johnson orders U.S. troops to carry out offensive operations to support South Vietnamese forces.

APRIL 7, 1965
President Johnson offers talks with North Vietnam.

APRIL 15, 1965
First demonstration against the war attracts sixteen thousand people in a march to the White House.

JUNE 19, 1965
Nguyen Cao Ky, the eighth South Vietnamese premier since Diem, is sworn in.

JULY 21–28, 1965
President Johnson raises the number of soldiers drafted to thirty-five thousand a month.

Below: *United States soldiers were given pocket guides to Vietnam to help them get to know the country.*

"I have asked the commanding general, General Westmoreland, what more he needs to meet this mounting aggression. He has told me. And we will meet his needs. We cannot be defeated by force of arms. We will stand in Vietnam. . . . I have today ordered to Vietnam the Air Mobile Division and certain other forces which will raise our fighting strength from seventy-five thousand to one hundred twenty-five thousand men almost immediately. Additional forces will be needed later, and they will be sent as requested.

"This will make it necessary to increase our active fighting forces by raising the monthly draft call from seventeen thousand over a period of time to thirty-five thousand per month and for us to step up our campaign for voluntary enlistments."

Address by President Johnson on television, July 28, 1965.

"June 7, 1968

Dear Mom and Dad

I am sorry for not writing. This is my fourteenth or fifteenth day in the field. I am on an operation south of Da Nang. The name of the operation is Allen Brook. Is there anything about it on the news? Its been going on since the twelfth of last month. So far, we've captured a lot of new weapons and tons of rice. June 5th things got a little rough on my company. We took twenty-eight wounded and six dead. So our company is hurting for some new men. On my birthday, things didn't go to good. One of my best friends, who I met in Hawaii, was shot twice in the stomach, and he died the following afternoon. His name was Art Sinksen . . . . I am so sick of fighting. I've seen and helped too many boys my age or younger that was wounded or dead. I thank the Lord each morning I get up. Well, I should be going on R&R [rest and recreation] any time. That's about it over here. So say hi to everyone, and take care of yourselves. Bye For Now.

All My Love
Your Son, Stephen

P.S. Write Soon"

A letter home from U.S. marine Stephen E. Austin

SEARCH-AND-DESTROY

Towards the end of 1966, General Westmoreland ordered the first of three large search-and-destroy missions. Operation Attleboro destroyed a key base camp northwest of Saigon, killing 3,130 communists and wounding 900, with 200 missing. In January 1967, Operation Cedar Falls was launched. Its aim was to seize control of an area northwest of Saigon known as the Iron Triangle. Troops were dropped in to evacuate the village of Ben Suc, and then an aerial bombardment took place, followed by a wave of ground troops. Underground tunnels were targeted and jungle was destroyed to remove cover. Despite these successes, enemy forces returned to the area soon after the soldiers left. This pattern was repeated after the final mission, Operation Junction City, when the enemy, who were used to local conditions, simply hid until the U.S. forces had left.

Right: *Both men and women fought for the NLF against United States and ARVN troops.*

"We slept in hammocks in small, thatched bamboo huts, and we held our meetings in deep underground tunnels, which also served as shelter against air raids. Informers in Saigon passed us intelligence, so we were able to decamp whenever the Americans and their South Vietnamese puppets planned operations in the area. Anyway, we could hear them coming, because big modern armies cannot move quietly. Still, we had some close shaves. Once, soon after I arrived, American airplanes dropped thousands of tons of bombs around us, but we weren't even scratched."

General Tran Do, North Vietnam army, from interview in Hanoi in 1981.

"You ask me what I thought of the Americans. We thought the Americans were handsome soldiers, but looked as if they were made with flour. . . . it was difficult for them to suffer all the hardships of the Vietnamese battle front. When we had no water to drink, they had water for showers! We could suffer the hardships much better than they could. That was probably the main reason we won."

A NVA soldier's opinion of U.S. soldiers, 1982.

Above: *Chip Parker with one of the ARA aircraft flown in the La Drang operation in November 1965.*

OCTOBER–NOVEMBER 1965
Battle of La Drang Valley takes place, the first major land battle of the conflict.

FEBRUARY 4, 1966
Televised hearings on the Vietnam War, headed by Senator J. William Fulbright, take place in the United States,

MARCH–APRIL 1966
A wave of protests against the South Vietnamese government, led by Buddhists and students, takes place.

JANUARY 8–26, 1967
Operation Cedar Falls takes place northeast of Saigon.

FEBRUARY 22–APRIL 1, 1967
Operation Junction City takes place.

SEPTEMBER 3, 1967
Nguyen Van Thieu becomes the new president of South Vietnam.

THE STRUGGLE MOVEMENT

In South Vietnam, public anger at the regime headed by Ky and Thieu was growing. The Struggle Movement, led by Buddhist monks and students, was furious at Ky's refusal to negotiate with Hanoi, his reluctance to include civilians in his government, and the army's ties to the United States. When government troops opened fire on protesters in Hue and Danang, calls for Ky to resign intensified. The fact that the United States supported Ky's actions did little to raise its own popularity. When the ARVN attacked Buddhist pagodas in May 1966, opposition broke out across the South and did not end until June. The way in which the Thieu government dealt with protesters turned many South Vietnamese against them, the United States, and the war itself.

Above: *One of millions of pins issued to try to raise support in the United States for the war in Vietnam.*

Western Union Telegram

--MR. AND MRS. ALBERT H. AUSTIN

4057 MAIN STREET, DENAIR CA

I DEEPLY REGRET TO CONFIRM THAT YOUR SON CORPORAL STEPHEN E. AUSTIN, USMC, DIED ON 8 JUNE 1968 IN THE VICINITY OF QUANG NAM, REPUBLIC OF VIETNAM. HE SUSTAINED GUNSHOT WOUNDS TO THE HEAD AND BODY FROM HOSTILE RIFLE FIRE WHILE ON AN OPERATION. THE FOLLOWING INFORMATION IS PROVIDED TO ASSIST YOU IN MAKING FUNERAL ARRANGEMENTS. HIS REMAINS WILL BE PREPARED, ENCASED, AND SHIPPED AT NO EXPENSE TO YOU, ACCOMPANIED BY AN ESCORT, EITHER TO A FUNERAL HOME OR TO A NATIONAL CEMETERY SELECTED BY YOU.

Telegram to the parents of U.S. marine Stephen E. Austin.

Above: *A scene from a "Teach-In" debate on President Johnson's policy in Vietnam that was broadcast to college campuses across the country in 1965.*

As more and more U.S. troops poured into Vietnam and as the number of casualties mounted, public sentiment against the war began to change. This change—coupled with the fact that no end to the conflict was in sight and little progress had been made by the United States on the battlefield—made many people think what had previously been unthinkable: For the first time, the United States might not win a war.

"I didn't make it all the way through the second tour because I was wounded for the second and third time. When I arrived home in California, I was treated like someone with the plague. I was spit on, yelled at, threatened, and looked upon as a mass murderer. Getting back to Medford was great because my family, friends, and neighbors were glad to see me in good health.

"If possible, and with the same political mindset that existed in the 60s, I wouldn't do it again. If this country were ever to be invaded or if our national interests were truly threatened, then yes, I would.

Gerald Cooper, a U.S. marine, interviewed in 1986.

ANTIWAR SENTIMENT

As President Johnson continued to pour troops into Vietnam, protesters against the war became more and more vocal. Soldiers returning home from the battlefield were astonished to find themselves being jostled by protesters, some of whom even spat at them. At a time of great upheaval in American society with issues such as civil rights and women's rights drawing a great deal of attention—protesting against U.S. involvement in Vietnam became for many people part of a wider questioning of American culture and government. When Johnson authorized Operation Rolling Thunder in the wake of the Gulf of Tonkin incident, a series of teach-ins was held across the country in protest. Many college professors, angry at Johnson's escalation of the war, held special lectures and classes to inform their students about what was happening in Vietnam. In 1967, a number of anti-war campaigns took place, including Negotiation Now!, a program of advertisements in national newspapers against the war; and Vietnam Summer, a antiwar effort that literally took the struggle to people's doorsteps. On October 21, a protest called the March on the Pentagon drew almost one hundred thousand people. Many protesters were involved in angry exchanges with police, and a watching Defense Secretary Robert McNamara was quoted as saying, "Christ, yes, I was scared." At the 1968 Democratic National Convention a riot broke out between protesters and police.

Below: *Protesters burning draft cards during an anti-Vietnam War demonstration in January 1967.*

THE DRAFT

The draft is a method by which the United States government can conscript fit civilians into the armed forces when there are shortages. In the Vietnam era, college students were exempted from the draft until 1969 There were also other ways of escaping service. These ranged from fleeing the country to failing the draft physical. Some people openly defied the draft. In protests across the country in October 1967, draft cards were burned, and resistors from New York sent defaced draft cards to the Attorney General in Washington.

On December 1, 1969, the possibility of being drafted literally became a lottery. The process of conscription changed from drafting the oldest man first to selecting civilians according to their date of birth. In front of television cameras, 366 plastic capsules (representing the 365 days of the year, plus a leap day) were put into a container and picked out by hand, to determine the order of call for all men between the ages of eighteen and twenty-six for the year of 1970. The lottery continued until all the days had been given order numbers. The draft lottery continued until 1973, when conscription ended.

LOSING HEARTS AND MINDS

Because of the difficulty of measuring territorial gains in Vietnam, a system called "body count" was adopted by the U.S. military to measure progress. This concern with the number of dead blurred the line between civilians and soldiers on the

---

"Thursday November 23rd
Dear Teri,

I'm sorry for not writing for such a long time. Now I am living in Toronto, Canada. I am married to a guy named Tom Connay. Boy, I know this is going to be all things you don't want to hear. We are living in Canada because Tom is a draft resistor. I respect his position immensely. We are planning to become Canadian citizens and renounce our American citizenship. . . .

Yours, Cynthia"

Cynthia Payne, wife of a draft resister, writing in 1968.

"I stood up to a screaming patriot and burned my draft card. I protested and marched, screamed and cried, told my generation to stop, don't go, this was wrong. I ended up a CO [conscientious objector] doing two years of bedpans, not smoking dope in Canada. I think that I, and those like me, are the true patriots, the true dissenters, who tried to stop fifty thousand of our generation from coming home in bags.

"Honor the resister, honor the protesters, the real patriots, those with the guts to stand up to a country gone mad with blood lust and a government hooked on body counts, and for what? Where is our memorial, where is our GI Bill for being right? 'Nam affected me, too, and changed my life, without being there. Think about it. Who was right? None of you HAD to go, you could have fought to stay home."

Excerpts from a Web site interview with Dr. Barry Spatz, 1992.

TIME LINE
1967

SEPTEMBER 29, 1967
President Johnson again offers talks with North Vietnam, promising to stop the bombing in return for talks. His proposition is called the "San Antonio Formula."

OCTOBER 16–21, 1967
Massive antidraft demonstrations take place in the United States. Folk singer Joan Baez is arrested in California.

OCTOBER 21–23, 1967
The March on the Pentagon attracts one hundred thousand demonstrators in Washington, D.C.

Above: This 1970s poster attracted thousands of antiwar protesters to a rally in New York.

Above: *The My Lai atrocity, in which U.S. soldiers massacred hundreds of unarmed villagers, turned many people against the United States' actions in Vietnam.*

battlefield. Some platoons adopted the slogan, "If it's dead and Vietnamese, it's VC." This casual attitude to life was one of many factors that made some Americans deeply concerned about the morality of the conflict. When an American platoon led by Lieutenant William Calley slaughtered 347 unarmed civilians at My Lai on March 16, 1968, people around the world felt revulsion. Soldiers' own accounts tell how women, children, the elderly, and even babies were killed by marauding soldiers. Calley was convicted of murder on March 29, 1971, but the massacre left an indelible mark on the consciousness of the American public. Some soldiers claimed that to understand how such a thing could happen, a person needed to experience the abuse suffered at boot camp. In the words of John Ketwig, men in boot camp were "pushed, pulled, beaten, screamed at, humiliated, and emasculated for eight weeks." Some claimed that this boot camp could brutalize a man to the point that he became capable of committing atrocities such as the My Lai massacre.

THE TET OFFENSIVE

At the beginning of 1968, troops from North Vietnam launched massive attacks on the South during Tet, Vietnam's most important holiday. The intention was to stop U.S. bombing, force the collapse of the South Vietnamese government and maybe even force U.S. withdrawal from Vietnam. The "Tet" strategy was to lure U.S. troops into the countryside as a diversion, and then launch major attacks on the cities, in the hope of causing their populations to rebel and join the

Above: *U.S. troops were issued guidebooks that told them exactly how they should behave during war. For some soldiers, many of the rules in these books seemed to be lost in the battlefields of Vietnam.*

"Hi everybody,
In one of your last letters, you wanted to know more about the country. Well, scenery wise, the country is beautiful, except for the barbwire and bunkers spread out all over the countryside. The people themselves . . . make me sick. You learn not to trust them. I've been shot at by too many innocent looking people to have any mercy. They learn to fire a rifle even before they walk . . . ."

Paul O'Connoll, a U.S. marine, December 2, 1968

"I had heard of the dedication and focus of the enemy at all levels but to actually see it and finally to be shocked by an event on the battlefield was more than a "mind blower". It was THE moment in time that solidified my opposition to the position that the Old Men in the government had put us in. We had no prayer of doing anything positive in that country because the enemy was everyone—everyone either hated us or just wanted to be left alone to grow their rice. We should just fold up our money and go home."

Marshall Darling, First Air Cavalry, Khe Sanh Valley, 1968.

> "This is to notify you that an offensive and uprising will take place in the very near future, and we will mount stronger attacks on towns and cities . . . . The enemy will be thrown into utmost confusion. No matter how violently the enemy may react, he cannot avoid collapse. This is not only a golden opportunity to liberate hamlets and villages but also an opportunity to liberate district seas, province capitals and South Vietnam as a whole. . . . Our victory is close at hand. The conditions are ripe. Our Party has carefully judged the situation. We must act and act fast. This is an opportunity to fulfil the aspirations of the entire people, of cadre, of each comrade, and of our families. . . ."

Directive to Communist forces for Tet Offensive, November, 1, 1967.

TIME LINE
1967–1968

DECEMBER 1967
General Westmoreland declares, "The enemy has been defeated at every turn."

**JANUARY 20–
APRIL 14, 1968**
North Vietnamese troops attack U.S. Khe Sanh base.

JANUARY 30, 1968
Tet Offensive begins. North Vietnamese and NLF forces attack South Vietnamese cities.

MARCH 16, 1968
A U.S. platoon kills hundreds of civilians at My Lai.

MAY 12, 1968
Peace talks between the U.S. and North Vietnam begin in Paris.

communist cause. NVA forces attacked the U.S. Marine Corps base at Khe Sanh in northwest South Vietnam on January 21. Johnson responded just as Ho Chi Minh had hoped he would, sending thousands of troops to defend the base, backed up by B-52 bombers. While this was happening, Northern forces attacked cities across the South. U.S. and ARVN forces fought back and eventually managed to subdue the communists. Although the U.S. forces appeared to come out on top, the number of U.S. soldiers who perished in the offensive made the American public realize how bloody the war was. The North Vietnamese leader General Giap summed up the situation by saying that, until Tet, the American people thought U.S. forces could win the war, but "now they knew that they could not."

SCALING DOWN

The bloodshed at Tet brought about a shift in American policy. President Johnson made a speech saying that bombing in North Vietnam would be restricted, and that the United States would negotiate with Hanoi. Talks between representatives of both sides were initiated and continued for the next five years. Despite this, in early 1968, U.S. operations in South Vietnam accelerated as Johnson

Right: The red arrows show the decoy attacks that preceded the Tet Offensive and the jagged circles indicate the main battles of the actual offensive.

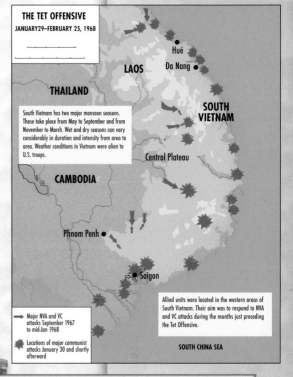

THE TET OFFENSIVE
JANUARY29–FEBRUARY 25, 1968

LAOS
Hué
Da Nang
THAILAND
SOUTH VIETNAM

South Vietnam has two major monsoon seasons. These take place from May to September and from November to March. Wet and dry seasons can vary considerably in duration and intensity from area to area. Weather conditions in Vietnam were alien to U.S. troops.

Central Plateau

CAMBODIA

Phnom Penh
Saigon

➡ Major NVA and VC attacks September 1967 to mid-Jan 1968

✳ Locations of major communist attacks January 30 and shortly afterward

Allied units were located in the western areas of South Vietnam. Their aim was to respond to NVA and VC attacks during the months just preceding the Tet Offensive.

SOUTH CHINA SEA

Right: NVA troops resting during the Tet Offensive.

Above: *U.S. marines exchange fire with enemy forces during the Tet Offensive in 1968.*

Below: *A map showing the U.S. invasion route into Cambodia.*

became increasingly fearful that the South Vietnamese government would collapse. Efforts to encourage South Vietnamese forces to take on a greater share of the fighting met with limited success, because they were increasingly unmotivated and reluctant to fight in a war that many were not sure why they were fighting.

NIXON AND NEGOTIATION

Although he had previously been a firm supporter of the Vietnam War and a politician renowned for his anticommunist views, Richard Nixon's election as president in 1968 ushered in the beginning of the end of the conflict. The bloodshed during Tet and the reaction to it in the United States convinced Nixon to run for election on a platform of "peace with honor." The plan was to engineer an honorable exit that would leave the South Vietnamese to stand firm against the communists, a shifting of responsibility Nixon called "Vietnamization." Between 1969 and 1971, while announcing troop withdrawals to the American public, Nixon used his "madman" theory—an effort to make Ho Chi Minh think that he might do anything to win the war—to try to force Hanoi to negotiate. He hoped that this plan might allow him to achieve the best peace terms possible. The first stage of Nixon's strategy was the bombing of the Ho Chi Minh Trail and secret attacks on Vietnamese bases in Cambodia. Then, when a pro-U.S. faction led by Lon Nol seized power in Cambodia, Nixon decided to send up to thirty thousand U.S. and ARVN troops across the border to aid Nol's fight against North Vietnamese insurgents while also

BATDAMBANG

CAMBODIA

KAMPONG THUM

PHNOM PENH

SAIGON

"April 1, 1969

Dear Professor Coffman,

How odd of me it is not to have written to you before this. . . . As the months have gone by (seven now) I've been trying to compare what I read in the American and foreign press to what I've actually observed. My position is . . . this is a war begun strictly by political elements in the American Congress. The authorization they receive to act under the Gulf of Tonkin resolution was artificially expanded to pronounce a mandate of military measures. In short, there was much pressure on Congress into letting them flex a little muscle. The Vietnamese are an illiterate people, who have little sense of Nationhood. They do not care to die for a cause which appears imposed by Westerners. . . . Therefore, the desertion rate is still horrendously high. Most of my good friends here feel that their sacrifice is not appreciated. As for the Saigon government, I personally feel that it will not last there after we have gone. . . . Vietnam has not been worth the price. War has never been productive, and our investment here will reap very little return.

Heroically yours, Benjamin"

Letter to University of Wisconsin-Madison
history professor Edward Coffman from a former student.

mounting an attack on the COSVN, a supposed Vietnamese communist office in Cambodia. The invasion of Cambodia led to protests on several university campuses in the United States, two of which ended in tragedy. On May 4, 1970, the National Guard shot dead four antiwar protesters at Kent State University, in Ohio. Then, on May 14, two students at Jackson State University, in Mississippi, were killed by police. Nixon's response to the outrage that followed was to announce that all U.S. troops would be pulled out of Cambodia by June. But this did not stop Nixon from extending the war again in February of 1971. Against the advice of General Westmoreland, Nixon sent ARVN troops supported by U.S. air power into Laos to attack North Vietnamese insurgents. The invasion was a disaster. The ARVN forces were decimated, raising doubts as to whether the South Vietnamese could win a war against the North without the United States.

THE PENTAGON PAPERS

In 1971, Nixon suffered a further blow when government documents known as the Pentagon Papers were leaked to *The New York Times* and *The Washington Post*. Commissioned by Robert McNamara in early 1967, these documents detail decision-making during the Vietnam War.

"How long would it take to succeed in Vietnam? They didn't know. How many more troops would it take? They couldn't say. Were two hundred thousand the answer? They weren't sure. Might they need more? Yes, they might need more. Could the enemy build up in exchange? Probably. So what was the plan to win the war? Well, the only plan was that attrition would wear out the Communists, and they would have had enough. Was there any indication that we've reached that point? No, there wasn't."

Defense secretary Clark M. Clifford speaking to Stanley Karnow about war plans just before the Tet Offensive.

They showed that U.S. leaders had broken international agreements, manipulated the South Vietnamese government, and lied to Congress and the American public about how badly the war was going. Nixon's chance of being reelected in the 1972 presidential elections seemed slim.

TIME LINE
1969–1970

MARCH 18, 1969
President Nixon begins policy of "Vietnamization."

SEPTEMBER 2, 1969
Ho Chi Minh dies.

MARCH 27, 1970
ARVN forces attack Communist bases in Cambodia.

MAY 4, 1970
Four protesters are killed at Kent State University by Ohio National Guard troops.

Left: *Student Mary Ann Vecchio kneels over the body of fellow student Jeffrey Miller, who was shot by National Guard troops during an antiwar protest at Kent State University, in Ohio.*

B y the middle of 1972 the United States government was coming to the realization that the war in Vietnam could not be won. Equally, the North Vietnamese were eager to break the stalemate that had existed in the country since the Tet Offensive. With both sides seemingly ready to compromise, the stage was set for negotiation. By the beginning of 1973, a deal had been made under which all United States troops would leave Vietnam by the end of the year.

"The United States and all other countries respect the independence, sovereignty, unity, and territorial integrity of Vietnam as recognized by the 1954 Geneva Agreements on Vietnam." (Article 1)

"A cease-fire shall be observed throughout South Vietnam as of 2400 hours, GMT, on January 27th, 1973." (Article 2)

"The United States will not continue its military involvement or intervene in the internal affairs of South Vietnam." (Article 4)

"The South Vietnamese people shall decide themselves the political future of South Vietnam through genuinely free and democratic general elections under international supervision." (Article 9)

Extracts from the Paris Peace Agreement, January 27, 1973.

THE ROAD TO PARIS

Four years after the Tet Offensive, General Giap ordered another massive invasion of South Vietnam in an attempt to end the war. The Easter Offensive saw more than one hundred thousand troops pour southward, hoping to overwhelm an enemy still shaken by the events in Laos. Despite initial successes, however, North Vietnam's hopes for a quick victory were dashed by a massive U.S. retaliatory bombing campaign called Operation Linebacker. With a stalemate continuing, both sides were beginning to realize that a diplomatic solution might be the only way to resolve the situation. Following secret talks between top officials from both sides, Le Duc Tho's "framework for peace"—a cease-fire followed by U.S. withdrawal—was approved by Nixon's national security advisor, Henry Kissinger, and plans were made to make the agreement official after Nixon's reelection. But when South Vietnam objected to the terms

Below: *Even after the cease-fire, fighting continued in South Vietnam.*

Above: *American prisoners of war reporting to U.S. representatives at Gia Lam Airport in Hanoi.*

TIME LINE
1971–1973

FEBRUARY 8, 1971
South Vietnamese troops begin an unsuccessful campaign to cut off the Ho Chi Minh Trail in Laos.

JUNE 13, 1971
The Pentagon Papers are published by *The New York Times*.

DECEMBER 26, 1971
President Nixon orders troops to start bombing North Vietnam again.

MARCH 30–APRIL 8, 1972
The Easter Offensive begins.

OCTOBER 8–11, 1972
Kissinger and Le Duc Tho agree on a deal to end the war, but it is rejected by South Vietnam.

DECEMBER 18–31, 1972
The U.S. Christmas bombing begins.

of the plan, Kissinger put forward amendments which resulted in talks being temporarily abandoned. Nixon sent aircraft and armored vehicles to the South to put pressure on Thieu to renegotiate, followed up by bombing of Hanoi and Haiphon on December 18. The two sides eventually resumed negotiations, and on January 27, 1973, the Paris Agreement was signed. While it signaled an end to the U.S. presence in Vietnam, the agreement failed to provide any clarity as to the precarious future of South Vietnam.

U.S. WITHDRAWAL

The number of U.S. troops in South Vietnam began to dwindle even before the Paris Agreement was signed, but the speed of their departure accelerated during 1973. South Vietnam released twenty-seven thousand prisoners of war, while North Vietnam released 591 American prisoners of war and more

"February 12 was a beautiful day in North Vietnam, at least to 112 American POWs. We had received our going away clothes the night before and cleaned up our rooms as wellas we could. We assembled in the courtyard and made our way under guard to the gate of the Hanoi Hilton. This was the first time we had moved anywhere from there without being blindfolded and handcuffed."

Excerpt from *Seven Years in Hanoi*, by Larry Chesley.
Larry Chesley was a POW for almost eight years.

Above: *President Nixon was reelected 1972, but he resigned in disgrace 1974 as a result of the Watergate scandal.*

"Today, with boundless joy, throughout the country our forty-five million people are jubilantly celebrating the great victory we have won in the general offensive and uprising this spring of 1975, in completely defeating the war of aggression and the neocolonialist rule of U.S. imperialism, liberating the whole of the southern half of our country so dear to our hearts and gloriously ending the longest, most difficult, and greatest patriotic war ever waged in the history of our people's struggle against foreign aggression. . . . We hail the new era in our nation's four thousand year history—era of brilliant prospects for the development of a peaceful, independent, reunified, democratic, prosperous, and strong Vietnam, an era in which the laboring people have become the complete masters of their destiny and will pool their physical and mental efforts to build a plentiful and happy life for themselves and for thousands of generations to come."

Le Duan's victory speech in Hanoi, May 15, 1975.

a policy he called the "Four No's." Senior figures in the South remained fearful about Nixon's commitment to protect the right of self-determination in South Vietnam. At the same time, appalling economic conditions in South Vietnam and antigoverment demonstrations by Buddhists and other groups further weakened the position of the Saigon government. Believing that the U.S. authorities might not protect Saigon, Thieu ordered NVA troops to head southward. After gaining Phuoc Long in the highlands and then Pleiku and Kontum, North Vietnamese troops could be found throughout the South.

The South Vietnamese army fell apart, and hundreds of thousands of refugees tried to flee. The decision not to intervene was made by the new president of the United States Gerald Ford, and the last Americans were whisked away from Saigon in helicopters as the communists

than five thousand South Vietnamese captives. A bill in Congress committed Nixon to withdrawing all troops by August 15. The only Americans left behind in Vietnam after this date would be civilians. In spite of this agreement, relations between North and South Vietnam remained as bad as ever. ARVN forces continued to fight throughout 1973 because Thieu refused to negotiate with communists, adopting

Below: *Vietnamese soldiers commemorate the twenty-fifth anniversary of the fall of the pro-United States regime in Saigon.*

Above: *A CIA employee helps evacuees onto an Air America helicopter from the top of 22 Gia Long Street, one-half of a mile from the U.S. Embassy.*

approached. It was a humiliating end to a war that had cost the lives of almost sixty thousand Americans and millions of Vietnamese from both sides of the divide. The jubilant Hanoi government renamed Saigon Ho Chi Minh City in memory of their most famous leader.

Right: *In February 1975, NVA troops began to flood southward.*

TIME LINE
1973–1975

JANUARY 23, 1973
President Nixon proclaims the signing of the Paris Agreement.

FEBRUARY 1973
American prisoners of war start to be released.

MARCH 1973
The last U.S. combat soldiers leave North Vietnam.

AUGUST 9, 1974
Nixon resigns after Watergate. President Ford takes charge.

FEBRUARY 1975
North Vietnamese offensive against Saigon begins.

APRIL 30, 1975
Saigon falls to communist forces. The Vietnam war is over.

"Saigon, South Vietnam, April 30 - Communist troops of North Vietnam and the Provisional Revolutionary Government of South Vietnam poured into Saigon today as a century of Western influences came to an end.

In Paris, representatives of the Provisional Revolutionary Government announced that Saigon had been renamed Ho Chi Minh City in honor of the late President of North Vietnam. Other representatives said in a broadcast monitored in Thailand that former Government forces in eight provinces south of the capital had not yet surrendered, but no fighting was mentioned.

The transfer of power was symbolized by the raising of the flag of the National Liberation Front over the presidential palace at 12:15 p.m. today, about two hours after General Minh's surrender broadcast."

The New York Times, April 30, 1975

 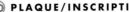

Beginning in the early 1960s, Vietnam loomed large in American culture. Television broadcasts about the war and films such as The Deer Hunter, Apocalypse Now, and the Rambo movies offered very different interpretations of the Vietnam War and its effects. Popular musicians ranging from Bob Dylan to Jimi Hendrix expressed their feelings about the war through their songs.

Below: *Robert De Niro starred as the mentally unstable Vietnam War veteran Travis Bickle in the 1976 film* Taxi Driver.

THE WAR ON FILM

Although films had been made about the troubles in Vietnam since the start of the war, large scale releases did not follow until the war had begun to draw toward its end. The war was increasingly unpopular with the American public, and as a result the subject was shunned by many Hollywood film makers. Then, in the 1970s, a series of films using the conflict as their subject were released. *Taxi Driver* (1976), while not exactly about the war, featured as its main character a returning veterna who was damaged and deranged. In Francis Ford Coppola's *Apocalypse Now* (1979), a man searches for a U.S. colonel who has disappeared in the jungles of Vietnam. When he finds him, he discovers a man who lives only to kill the North Vietnamese enemy, a figure on the brink of savagery. In the 1980s, the trilogy of Rambo movies, starring Sylvester Stallone, showed another trend in Vietnam films—raw-action war movies whose heroes fought not only a tangible enemy but a U.S. government that often withheld its support from those who would "get the job done." *Platoon*, released in 1986, dramatized the day-to-day life for soldiers in Vietnam, and in 1987, Stanley Kubrick's *Full Metal Jacket* looked at how the brutal shock of military boot camp and its culture could make some men capable of committing war atrocities. More recently, Oliver Stone's *Born on the Fourth of July* (1989)—based on a book by Ron Kovic, a disabled veteran—reflected the changing public view of Vietnam veterans. In Stone's film, Kovic suffers humiliation at boot camp and terrible injury on the battlefield, and returns to rejection at home, only finding redemption and acceptance more than a decade later when the public began to realize the bravery of the veterans who had fought for the United States. The

> "Day by day I struggle to maintain not only my strength but also my sanity. It's all a blur. I have no energy to write. I don't know what is right or wrong anymore. The morale of the men is low, a civil war in the platoon.
>
> Somebody once wrote: 'Hell is the impossibility of reason.' That's what this place feels like. Hell."
>
> (Chris Taylor)
>
> **Excerpt from the film *Platoon* (1986), directed by Oliver Stone.**

Above: *The slogan for Oliver Stone's 1986 film* Platoon—"The first casualty of war is innocence"— *expressed the moral problems many soldiers faced in Vietnam.*

APRIL 30, 1975
The U.S. trade embargo is extended to cover all Vietnam.

JULY 1976
Vietnam is formally reunified. More than six hundred thousand people are moved from Ho Chi Minh City (formerly Saigon) to rural areas in a resettlement plan.

DECEMBER 1978
Vietnam invades Cambodia and topples Pol Pot's Khmer Rouge government, ending its reign of terror.

1979
Western European countries and noncommunist Asian nations support a U.S.-led embargo against Vietnam in protest of Vietnam's invasion of Cambodia.

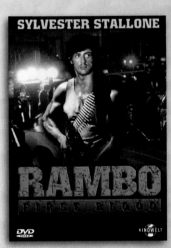

Above: *The DVD cover of the 1982 film that stars Sylvester Stallone as the persecuted Vietnam veteran John Rambo.*

"In the last month of school, the marine recruiters came and spoke to my senior class . . . . It was like all the movies and all the books and all the dreams of becoming a hero come true. 'Good afternoon, men,' the tall marine said. 'We have come today because they told us that some of you want to become marines.' He told us that the marines took nothing but the best. . . . The tall marine spoke in a very beautiful way about the exciting history of the marines and how they had never lost and America had never been defeated. . . . As I shook their hands and stared up into their eyes, I couldn't help but feel I was shaking hands with John Wayne and Audie Murphy."

Excerpt from *Born on the Fourth of July*, by Ron Kovic.

Below: *Bob Dylan was a key figure in the antiwar movement.*

Vietnam War was also captured on film by North Vietnamese cameramen. Numerous documentaries not released in the West were shown in Vietnam and other communist countries. Today, there are plans to make many of these films available to people outside Vietnam for the first time.

THE WAR ON VINYL

From the moment the conflict in Vietnam began, popular music in the United States began to reflect the tensions it provoked. Famous protest songs of the era included "Last Train to Clarksville," by The Monkees, which is about a man on his way to an army base, knowing he may die in Vietnam ("I don't know if I'm ever coming home") and Creedence Clearwater Revival's

"Fortunate Son," the tale of a working-class soldier unable to dodge the draft because he "ain't no Senator's son." Protest through music continued at the Woodstock festival, held in 1969. Many of the artists who performed at Woodstock, including Joan Baez and Country Joe, made antiwar speeches. After the Kent State University shootings in 1970, "Ohio," by Crosby, Stills, Nash, and Young, angrily attacked the actions of the National Guard. Not all musicians, however, were against the war. Artists including Johnny Cash stood up for the soldiers fighting in Vietnam, saluting their bravery in defending their country and criticizing the actions of the protesters who jeered them upon their return.

ARTISTS AND THE WAR

Art also played an important role in shaping opinions during the war. During the Vietnam War, the U.S. Army sent teams of soldier-artists into the field to create a visual record of their experiences. Their art is now on display in the U.S. Army's Center

"I got a friend named Whiskey Sam

He was my boonierat buddy for a year in Nam

He said is my country just a little off track

Took 'em twenty-five years to welcome me back

It was a real slow walk in a real sad rain

And nobody tried to be John Wayne

I came home, but Tex did not

And I can't talk about the hit he got

I got a little limp now when

I walk Got a little tremolo when

I talk But my letter read from Whiskey Sam

You're a walkin' talkin' miracle from Vietnam"

"Drive On," by Johnny Cash (1963).

"How many roads must a man walk down

Before you call him a man?

Yes, 'n' how many seas must a white dove sail

Before she sleeps in the sand?

Yes, 'n' how many times must the cannonballs fly

Before they're forever banned?

The answer, my friend, is blowin' in the wind,

The answer is blowin' in the wind."

"Blowin' in the Wind," by Bob Dylan (1963).

Above: *An oil painting by R.G. Smith showing three Vietnamese people awaiting questioning on the deck of a patrol boat.*

TIME LINE
1979–1982

FEBRUARY 1979
Suspicious of Vietnamese relations with the Soviet Union after the Treaty of Friendship and Cooperation in 1978, China decides to invade Vietnam.

1982
About one hundred twenty thousand former members of the deposed Saigon regime, plus critics of the new government and other minorities, are held in "re-education camps."

MARCH 1982
Vietnamese Communist Party (VCP) holds its Fifth National Party Congress, in which leaders admit mistakes have been made in rebuilding the country.

of Military History. Navy combat artists also recorded the scenes they witnessed.

The war also provided inspiration for satirical artists around the world. Cartoonists such as Herblock (Herbert Block) of *The Washington Post* published weekly cartoons that called public attention to what was happening in Vietnam. Herblock's cartoons frequently were highly critical of both U.S. policies in Vietnam and the actions of presidents such as Richard Nixon.

Below: *This satirical cartoon by Herblock, published August 9, 1972, mocks Nixon's 1968 promise to end the war in Vietnam.*

HEADQUARTERS
20TH GENERAL SUPPORT GROUP
US ARMY ASCOM DISTRICT
APO SAN FRANCISCO 96220

Sp instr: Upon completion of TDY in Vietnam EM is placed on 75 days dy w/SSO, Hq USARHAW, APO SF 96557... Indiv must havein poss basic req summer unif, work unif & cbt boots. Plague immun req but tvl WNB delayed except for 1st vaccine dose. Bording pass DA Form 1472 will be reequ for MAC flight overseas. Indiv WB equip w/m17 protective mask & corr lenses if nec prior to dprt this comd. ID tags WB worn while tvl by mil aircraft. Indiv w/have cy of immun rec & valid ID card in poss at all times. Bag alw 66 lbs; personal eff, and an ex bag alw of 30 lbs for art supplies and technical equip. Combat pay of $65.00 per month will be auth while on duty in Vietnam. Per diem will be in accord with JTR.

This telegram authorizes the supplying of art materials to a soldier artist serving in Vietnam.

Above: *This certificate recognizes the bravery of Canadian Lawrence M. Dickens, who helped to rescue Vietnamese "boat people."*

Thirty years after the end of the Vietnam war, the war continues to provoke debate in the United States and around the world. After U.S. troops left Vietnam, the battered and bombed country had to begin the process of rebuilding. Back home, veterans had to take their places in society, and the United States had to take another look at its position in the world. Today, relations between the United States and Vietnam have been restored, but the issue of Vietnam has not disappeared.

THE LEGACY IN VIETNAM

After their victory, which reunified Vietnam, the Hanoi government had to piece together a country badly bruised and divided by the war. For the next twenty years, the country would be one of the poorest in the world, due to the damage inflicted by the war and also the disastrous economic policies implemented by the communist regime. In neighboring Cambodia, the U.S.-backed Lon Nol government collapsed, and the Khmer Rouge rose to power and commited a genocide that claimed the lives of 1.7 million people, or about 26 percent of the population. When hundreds of thousands of Cambodian refugees poured over the border to Vietnam, the Hanoi government decided to invade Cambodia, provoking an attack from China, Cambodia's ally. Vietnam found itself isolated internationally and drawn into a bloodbath that cost the lives of more than fifty thousand Vietnamese people by the time troops finally left Cambodia in 1991.

"Affected areas covered 75 miles [120 kilometers] east-west and 93 miles [150 kilometers] north-south. Five minutes was all that was needed to wither tapioca, sweet potato . . . and banana plants. Livestock suffered heavy injuries. . . . Most of the river fish were found lying dead on the surface of mountain streams and brooks. The three days of chemical attack poisoned scores of people, took the lives of about ten and inflicted a "natus" disease (with symptoms like a severe rash) upon eighteen thousand inhabitants."

A Vietnamese peasant describing a three-day chemical attack near Da Nang in February 1966.

Right: *A U.S. plane drops the chemical Agent Orange over a North Vietnamese jungle. Agent Orange was used to kill foliage under which enemy troops may have been hiding.*

A POISONED LANDSCAPE?

The war in Vietnam left a deadly legacy that stayed long after U.S. troops went home. U.S. forces sprayed Agent Orange, a chemical cocktail containing the poison dioxin, over the jungle to remove cover under which Viet Cong troops might hide. Today, the rates of cancer in Vietnam are much higher than in surrounding countries, and doctors attribute this to the effects of Agent Orange. The chemical also had a highly damaging effect on farming because areas stripped by Agent Orange were later overrun by weeds. Another dangerous legacy of the war are the land mines that are still hidden around the country. In some places, the ground is studded with unexploded bombs and shells that can explode when land is farmed, cleared, or walked over.

PERSECUTED PEOPLE

Between 1975 and 1990, more than one million frightened Vietnamese fled the country, many seeking refuge in the United States. Some were so desperate to escape that they left Vietnam in tiny fishing boats to sail to freedom, gaining the name "boat people." Many of those South Vietnamese who stayed in Vietnam found themselves persecuted by the new regime because of their collaberation with United States troops. Hundreds of thousands of South Vietnamese were imprisoned and tortured by the communist authorities or sent to concentration camps. Employment prospects for people from South

Right: After U.S. forces left Vietnam, thousands of "boat people" fled the country because they feared the new communist regime.

"I saw hundreds of people trying to escape the thick black smoke rising up into the gray sky. All our homes, the entire village, was in flames. People had grabbed what belongings they could carry before they left. Some had bicycles to carry their possessions, others had baskets or push carts. Little children were carried by older brothers and sisters or pulled along by harassed mothers, arms full of bundles.

"When we got into the boat, I liked watching fish swimming in the water and all the boats around us. It was like an adventure for me. I did not understand what was really happening. My mom was holding my little sister, and she was crying, but I didn't understand, I was too excited."

Anh and Kim's account of their escape from Vietnam.

TIME LINE
1982–1987

NOVEMBER 11, 1982
The Vietnam Veterans' Memorial, known as "the Wall," is dedicated in Washington, D.C.

1985
The Hanoi government says it is still holding ten thousand inmates in "re-education" camps. Some people believe the actual number is forty thousand. Ho Chi Minh City mayor Mai Chi Tho tells Western reporters that "socialist transition" will not be complete until 2000.

AUGUST 1–3, 1987
A special envoy of U.S. president Ronald Reagan, General John Vesey, visits Vietnam to discuss humanitarian issues of interest to both countries.

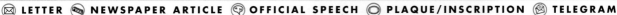

Above: *Many people who left Vietnam settled in the United States and had children. These Amerasian young women are a reminder of the history between Vietnam and the United States.*

Below: *The Vietnam Veterans Memorial wall was dedicated in November 1982. The tradition of leaving gifts at the base of "the wall" began before it was even completed.*

Vietnamese families that had helped the U.S. forces were also severely hampered because the new regime forced them to declare this fact when applying for jobs. For the many Vietnamese women who gave birth to children conceived in relationships with U.S. soldiers during the war, life in the new Vietnam was even harder. Mixed-race children were given the names "con lai" ("half-breed") or "bui doi" ("the dust of life"), while their mothers were frowned upon in Vietnamese society. In the words of Mai Thi Kim, the mother of an Amerasian child: "When you gave birth to a mixed kid, in the countryside, they hold many prejudice against you." Because it was very difficult to leave Vietnam after 1975, the option of joining their fathers in the United States was not available. In 1987, however, with relations improving between the United States and Vietnam, the U.S. congress passed the Amerasian Homecoming Act. By 1994, twenty-five thousand Amerasians had arrived in the United States.

VIETNAM VETS AND THE WALL

When U.S. forces returned from the war, many found it very hard to settle back into civilian life. Some suffered mental illnesses as a result of what they had experienced in the jungles of Southeast Asia and had to cope in a society which, at first, showed little sympathy for their plight. Those in need of medical help often found themselves treated harshly by doctors. Divorce, alcoholism, and even homelessness remain common among Vietnam veterans. It is estimated that about one-quarter of all homeless people on the streets of the United States are Vietnam veterans. In 1982, however, the U.S. government took a major step toward showing appreciation for the Vietnam veterans: the building of the Vietnam Veterans Memorial in Washington, D.C. Designed by Maya Ying Lin, it bears the names of 58,325 U.S. soldiers killed in Vietnam.

THE MIA ISSUE

After the war ended, many U.S. soldiers who had fought could not be

The wall begins on panel 1E with the following inscription: "IN HONOR OF THE MEN AND WOMEN OF THE ARMED FORCES OF THE UNITED STATES WHO SERVED IN THE VIETNAM WAR. THE NAMES OF THOSE WHO GAVE THEIR LIVES AND OF THOSE WHO REMAIN MISSING ARE INSCRIBED IN THE ORDER THEY WERE TAKEN FROM US" From panel 1E to panel 70E, which is dated May 25, 1968, the East wall appears to recede into the ground. It resumes at the end of the West wall at panel 70W. The West wall appears to emerge from the ground, continuing at May 25, 1968, and ending with the panel dated 1975, with the inscription: "OUR NATION HONORS THE COURAGE, SACRIFICE AND DEVOTION TO DUTY AND COUNTRY OF ITS VIETNAM VETERANS. THIS MEMORIAL WAS BUILT WITH PRIVATE CONTRIBUTIONS FROM THE AMERICAN PEOPLE. NOVEMBER 11, 1982"

The Vietnam Veterans Memorial wall, Washington, D.C.

"Thank you for your letter concerning Prisoners of War and Missing in Action service members. Your accounting of Wade Lynn Ellen is tragic and, as you concluded, is an unfinished event that deserves to be resolved.

There have been several initiatives before the 106th Congress to address the issue of Prisoners of War and Missing in Action service members. These measures include:

House Concurrent Resolution 311: Expresses the sense of Congress that the United States should continue to actively pursue efforts to achieve a full accounting of all members of the Armed Forces who remain unaccounted for from previous conflicts, particularly the Korean War and the Vietnam War, and to continue and maintain programs and procedures for achieving a full accounting of all military personnel who become prisoners of war or missing in action in future conflicts.

Once again I thank you for contacting me on this very important matter, and I am moved by the concern and compassion you displayed for a fellow American.

Kind Regards,
Senator Warner"

August 23, 2000 ~ Response from Senator John Warner

found. They were categorized as "MIA," or "missing in action." A survey taken shortly after the war showed that many Americans thought that MIA soldiers might still be imprisoned in North Vietnam. Teams of Americans were sent to Vietnam to search for them or their remains. The authorities in Hanoi allowed this in the hope of encouraging better relations between the two countries. Some ordinary Vietnamese, however, were offended when Americans dug up graves in cemeteries, disturbing the bodies of their relatives in the process. Today, only a few Americans still believe that U.S. soldiers continue to be held in North Vietnam.

Below: *U.S. servicemen and women carry a coffin containing the remains of a soldier recovered in Vietnam's central provinces. About eighteen hundred U.S. personnel are listed as missing in action.*

TIME LINE
1988–1995

SEPTEMBER 29, 1990
Foreign Minister Nguyen Co Thach meets Secretary of State James Baker in New York.

NOVEMBER 11, 1991
The U.S. government officially allows American tourists, veterans, journalists, businessmen to visit Vietnam.

NOVEMBER 1994
President Bill Clinton visits Hanoi and receives a warm welcome. The United States embargo on Vietnam is lifted the same year.

JANUARY 27, 1995
The United States and Vietnam establish liaison offices in each other's capitals.

JULY 11, 1995
President Clinton announces the normalization of relations with Vietnam.

Below: *Many Vietnam veterans— no longer made to feel ashamed of their involvement in the war—wear badges that show that they served in Vietnam.*

Below: *American veteran of the Vietnam war Bill Dyke hugs his former enemy, retired North Vietnamese army soldier Mai Thuan, during a groundbreaking meeting between veterans from both sides of the Vietnam War, in Hanoi, on April 26, 2000.*

RELATIONS WITH VIETNAM

The United States and Vietnam were not willing to consider repairing relations for many years after the war ended. When Vietnam invaded Cambodia, the United States, together with countries of Western Europe, placed a embargo on Vietnam. As recently as 1991, the United States prevented the International Monetary Fund (IMF) from granting economic aid to Vietnam. But by the 1980s, contact between the two nations had begun to grow, aided by Vietnam's cooperation on the MIA issue and Vietnam's withdrawal from Cambodia. In 1991, the United States and Vietnam agreed to establish an office in Hanoi to help to determine the fate of MIA soldiers, and the U.S. government gave Vietnam a road map toward the restoration of normal relations. Later that year, the United States lifted a ban on its citizens traveling to Vietnam. In 1994, President Clinton lifted the U.S. embargo on Vietnam. The following year, diplomatic relations resumed. Today, many Western tourists, including visitors from the United States, travel to Vietnam. Misunderstandings still occur—an American plan to open a chain called Uncle Ho's Hamburgers was not well received—but tourism is now one of the biggest industries in Vietnam.

U.S. FOREIGN POLICY

It can be argued that the Vietnam War had a distinct effect on U.S. foreign policy and made the United States more hesitant to commit its forces to missions around the world in the 1970s and 1980s. Public opinion during the 1980s remained resolutely against the United States becoming involved in "another Vietnam," and polls showed that most people were deeply concerned about possible U.S. military involvement in

"Had it not been for Vietnam, President Reagan would have had U.S. troops in Nicaragua and probably several other places. Because of Vietnam, the American people would have none of it, so it didn't happen. Those of us who think the Vietnam War was a terrible mistake should carefully consider how we feel about the Americans who fought there. We should take that thought one step further and realize that many individual soldiers were fighting for their country. They did heroic things for their country. They died for their country. A sacrifice for a cause you believe is right is no less a sacrifice because ten years later it turns out not to be right. Those soldiers' intent was to fight for their country, and that intent was noble."

Terry Crenshaw, a Vietnam protester posting on a Vietnam Web site in 1996.

Above: *Members of a crowd hold up signs protesting U.S. military intervention in the Middle East in the Gulf War.*

TIME LINE
1995–2003

AUGUST 5, 1995
U.S. embassy in Hanoi opened by Secretary of State Warren Christopher.

APRIL 10, 1997
Former POW Douglas "Pete" Peterson becomes the first ambassador to Vietnam since the end of the Vietnam War.

OCTOBER 3, 2001
The United States Senate approves an agreement normalizing trade between the United States and Vietnam.

NOVEMBER 10, 2003
U.S. secretary of defense Donald Rumsfeld meets Vietnam's defense minister Pham Van Tra.

NOVEMBER 19, 2003
Navy missile frigate USS *Vandegrift* docks at Ho Chi Minh City, in a symbolic act intended to improve relations between Vietnam and the United States.

Central America. It was not until the Gulf War in 1991 that the United States made another significant commitment of troops in a foreign country. Following victory, President George H. W. Bush's said, "By God, we've kicked the Vietnam syndrome once and for all!," showing a new outlook. The United States also sent forces to Kosovo in the 1990s; to Afghanistan in 2001; and to Iraq in 2003.

In U.S. politics, a Vietnam service record became a badge of honor rather than shame. Vietnam-era military service first emerged as an issue in the 1992 presidential race, when Bill Clinton was accused of draft dodging. In the 2000 presidential race, George W. Bush faced questions about whether he used family connections to avoid serving in Vietnam, and in the 2004 race, he was questioned about his record in the Texas National Guard. In contrast, Bush's 2004 opponent, John Kerry—who received three Purple Hearts while fighting in Vietnam—had a distinguished record in the U.S. Navy. His Vietnam war record confirmed his patriotism to many Americans.

Above: *Today visitors from the United States go to Vietnam as tourists, where they are welcomed by the Vietnamese people.*

"Beloved, I continue to feel the pain and anguish and loss as deeply as the day I was told you were gone. The new friends I have made, the McAninch family I have recovered, the restored letters and photographs to replace my lost mementos, the web sites I have created for you and them—all have provided solace and some respite for my aching heart. But when you went down into that Valley, when you went back to defend your Marine brothers, my hand was in yours: I went with you; I feel the mortar fragments searing my own chest and back every day, and I groan and rage against the pain and unfairness of your tragedy. Part of me, the best part of me, never returned from Vietnam either. Nothing, nothing can ever replace you in my life."

Letter from Joan McAninch to Michael McAninch, a marine killed in action in Vietnam in 1969.

CHAPTER 7

MAJOR FIGURES

The Vietnam War was run by major figures on both sides. For the United States, presidents Eisenhower, Kennedy, Johnson, and Nixon made major decisions about the war that changed the course of American history. On the Vietnamese side, leaders from both North Vietnam and South Vietnam shaped the conflict. The weakness of the leaders in South Vietnam and their treatment of their citizens often contrasted starkly with the North Vietnamese authorities and contributed to the eventual collapse of the country.

UNITED STATES LEADERS

President Eisenhower

President Dwight D. Eisenhower (right) was born in Texas in 1890. He had a distinguished military career, which included commanding the troops invading France on D-Day during World War II in 1944. Early in the Vietnam conflict, he decided against helping France at Dienbienphu, having previously supported them. Eisenhower was supportive of the Diem regime in South Vietnam, in spite of its unpopularity.

President Kennedy

President John F. Kennedy was born in Brookline, Massachusetts, in 1917. He was elected president in 1960 and, during his brief presidency, led the United States as a fierce opponent of communism. In the 1960s, Kennedy decided that "Vietnam was the place" to halt the spread of communism and sent U.S. forces to Vietnam to train Vietnamese soldiers. He was assassinated in 1963.

President Johnson

Lyndon B. Johnson was born in Texas in 1908. When President Kennedy was assassinated, Johnson, who was Kennedy's vice president, took over the presidency. He led the United States deeper into the Vietnam War with the bombing of North Vietnam and increased troop deployment in the country.

Robert McNamara

Robert McNamara was born in San Francisco in 1916. At the request of President-elect John F. Kennedy, McNamara agreed to serve as secretary of defense of the United States, a position he held from 1961 until 1968. He is known for commissioning the Pentagon Papers.

President Nixon

Richard Nixon was born in California in 1913. He served in the Eisenhower administration before being elected president in 1968. Despite promising to remove troops from Vietnam during the 1968 elections, a peace agreement was not signed until 1973.

Henry Kissinger

Born in Germany in 1923, Henry Kissinger came to the United States in 1938. He was appointed national security adviser by President Nixon in 1969, and he helped negotiate the Paris Agreement with Le Duc Tho in 1973.

SOUTH VIETNAMESE LEADERS

President Diem

Ngo Dinh Diem was born in Vietnam in 1901. After the Geneva conference in 1954, Diem became the new ruler of South Vietnam. He opposed communism, but after angering Buddhists with his heavy-handed policies and use of violence, President Diem was overthrown by a military coup in November 1963.

President Thieu

Nguyen Van Thieu was born on April 5, 1923, in Ninh Tvuan, in central Vietnam. He served in the French-supported Vietnam National Army from 1948 to 1954, fighting the pro-communist forces of Ho Chi Minh. Thieu became South Vietnam's head of state under Prime Minister Ky's government between 1965 and 1967. On September 3, 1967, Thieu became South Vietnam's president, a position he held until the communist victory in 1975.

NORTH VIETNAMESE LEADERS

Ho Chi Minh

Nguyen That Thanh was born in 1890 in central Vietnam. He became a passionate supporter of the Communist cause while living in Europe between 1915 and 1923. Thanh then moved to Hong Kong, where he founded the Vietnamese Communist Party. In 1941, Thanh created the Vietminh and changed his name to Ho Chi Minh, which means "He Who Enlightens." He proclaimed Vietnam independent from France in 1945, and he continued to fight the French and, later, the United States beginning in 1954. Ho Chi Minh stayed president of North Vietnam until his death in 1969.

General Giap

Born in 1911, Vo Nguyen Giap became one of the most important military figures in North Vietnam. General Giap made the People's Army of Vietnam (PAVN) into the force that defeated the French at Dien Bien Phu in May 1954. In the fight against the United States, Giap was the architect of the Tet Offensive. He retired in 1973, following the failed Easter Offensive. General Giap was given the Gold Star Order, Vietnam's highest decorative honor, in 1992.

President Le Duan

Le Duan was born in 1907, in central Vietnam. He joined the Communist Party as a young man, and by 1959, he was secretary general. Le Duan played a key role in the insurgency in South Vietnam. He was responsible for the creation of the People's Revolutionary Party in 1962, a key part of the National Liberation Front. Le Duan became leader of North Vietnam after Ho Chi Minh's death in 1969.

Le Duc Tho

Le Duc Tho was born in North Vietnam in 1911. Tho helped found the Indo-Chinese Communist Party in 1930. In 1945, Tho established the Vietnam Revolutionary League, or Vietminh, with Ho Chi Minh and Vo Nguyen Giap. Tho was in charge of the Vietminh until 1954, when he joined the the Communist Party of Vietnam. Tho continued to lead the insurgency in South Vietnam, while, at the same time, negotiating with Henry Kissinger in order reach a peace settlement. Le Duc Tho rejected the 1973 Nobel Peace Prize, which was awarded to himself and Kissinger jointly.

Agent Orange a spray containing dioxin, a toxic chemical, that was used to kill vegetation during the Vietnam War in order to reveal enemy hiding places.

Allies in World War II, the United States, Britain, France, and other countries that worked together to fight the Axis forces of Germany, Japan, and Italy.

Amerasian a person of mixed American and Asian heritage, especially the offspring of a father who was a U.S. serviceman in Asia and a Vietnamese mother.

ARVN the Army of the Republic of Vietnam, set up by Diem in South Vietnam to fight communists in North Vietnam.

assassinated murdered in a sudden and often secretly planned attack, usually for political reasons.

boat people Vietnamese refugees, mainly from the South, who fled the country after 1975 to escape persecution by the communist regime.

Buddhism a religion followed by many Vietnamese people that teaches that pain is inherent in life and that a person can be freed of this pain through moral and spiritual purification.

CIDG Civilian Irregular Defense Groups; groups set up with the help of the United States to provide surveillance in the mountains of Vietnam.

civilians people who are not members of an armed service group, police force, or firefighting force.

Cold War the hostile but nonviolent relationship between the United States and the Soviet Union and their respective allies that lasted from the end of World War II until the breakup of the Soviet Union.

communist having to do with an individual or government that advocates an economic system run by a dictatorship of the working class that strives for a society in which private property is abolished and all land and factories are collectively owned; a person who advocates communist government.

Congress the federal legislative body of the United States, consisting of the Senate and the House of Representatives.

conscripted enrolled into military service by compulsion.

coup a sudden use of force or pressure in politics, usually by a small group, that causes a change in government.

credible giving good reason to be believed.

democratic having a system of government where all of a country's population has a vote in choosing who runs that nation's government.

Eastern Bloc the communist countries of Eastern Europe.

genocide the organanized and deliberate killing of a racial, political, or cultural group.

guerrilla a member of a force that engages in the type of warfare, that involves the harassment of an army, usually by small groups.

ICP the Indochinese Communist Party, which was set up in Hong Kong in 1929 by Ho Chi Minh.

Iron Triangle the name during the Vietnam War for a region northwest of Saigon.

leap day an extra day (February 29) inserted in the calendar every four years, in order to keep the calendar in harmony with the rotation of the Earth.

MIA Missing in Action; the label given to soldiers unaccounted for after the end of the Vietnam war.

monk a man who belongs to a religious order and lives among other men who belong to the same group.

nationalist a person who favors or fights for the unity, independence, and interests of a particular country.

NLF National Liberation Front, or Viet Cong; the group formed by communist supporters in South Vietnam in 1960 to organize resistance efforts against the South Vietnamese government and the United States

NVA the North Vietnamese Army formed by Ho Chi Minh.

pagoda a tower built as a temple or a memorial that has upward-curving roofs at the divisions of each of its several stories.

PLAF People's Liberation Armed Forces; the group formed by communist supporters in South Vietnam in 1960 to run the military side of the conflict (*see also* NLF).

propaganda information and news presented and spread in such a way that it supports or opposes a particular political message.

Purple Heart the decoration awarded by the United States military to a soldier who has been wounded or killed in action.

republic a government in which supreme power is vested in the people and their elected representatives.

retaliatory done for the purpose of revenge.

reunify to rejoin something, such as a country, that has been divided.

satirical having to do with the use of wit, irony, or sarcasm to expose and discredit foolish behavior.

SEATO South East Asia Treaty Organization; the organization set up among the Unites States and a number of countries to protect Vietnam from aggression.

self-determination choice of their own political organization by the people of a geographical region.

Soviet Union also known as the Union of Soviet Socialist Republics, or USSR; the large communist country that, until it broke up in 1991, was made up of what are now the countries of Armenia, Azerbajian, Belarus, Estonia, Georgia, Kazakhstan, Kyrgyzstan, Latvia, Lithuania, Moldova, Russia, Tajikistan, Turkmenistan, Ukraine, and Uzbekistan.

Special Forces soldiers from a division of the U.S. Army who are trained for guerilla warfare.

stalemate a situation in which competing individuals or groups have reached a point at which it is clear that neither can win.

Tet the Vietnamese New Year holiday that begins at the second new moon after the winter solstice.

Vietminh Vietnamese nationalist organization set up by Ho Chi Minh.

vilify to speak abusively of a person in a way that falsely conveys the idea that person is the source of problems or evils.

Please visit our web site at: www.garethstevens.com
For a free color catalog describing Gareth Stevens Publishing's
list of high-quality books and multimedia programs,
call 1-800-542-2595 or 1-800-387-3178 (Canada).
Gareth Stevens Publishing's fax: (414) 332-3567.

Library of Congress Cataloging-in-Publication Data

Mason, Andrew, 1970-
    The Vietnam War: a primary source history / Andrew Mason.
        p. cm. — (In their own words)
    Includes bibliographical references and index.
    ISBN 0-8368-5981-2 (lib. bdg.)
    1. Vietnamese Conflict, 1961-1975—Juvenile literature. I. Title.
II. In their own words (Milwaukee, Wis.)
DS557.7M365   2005
959.704'33—dc22   2005040896

This North American edition first published in 2006 by
Gareth Stevens Publishing
A Member of the WRC Media Family of Companies
330 West Olive Street, Suite 100
Milwaukee, WI 53212 USA

This U.S. edition copyright © 2006 by Gareth Stevens, Inc.
Original edition copyright © 2005 ticktock Entertainment Ltd.
First published in Great Britain in 2005 by ticktock Media Ltd.,
Unit 2, Orchard Business Centre, North Farm Road,
Tunbridge Wells, Kent, TN2 3XF, U.K.

Gareth Stevens editorial direction: Mark J. Sachner
Gareth Stevens art direction: Tammy West
Gareth Stevens designer: Jenni Gaylord

Photo credits: (b=bottom; c=center; l=left; r=right; t=top)
CORBIS: 2 & 23(b), 4-5, 7(all), 8-9(c), 14(b), 15(t), 16(b), 20(b), 20(t),
26(b), 27(t), 28(b), 29(t), 34-35, 37(b), 38-39(all). Everett Collection: 30l,
31(t). Getty Images: 6(t),12(b), 13(b), 22(t), 25(b), Magnum Photos: 9(b).

Every effort has been made to trace the copyright holders. We
apologize in advance for any unintentional omissions. We would be
pleased to insert the appropriate acknowledgments in any subsequent
edition of this publication.

Printed in the United States of America

1 2 3 4 5 6 7 8 9 09 08 07 06 05